MEGA BOOKS

CARS

CHRISTIANE GUNZI

Gareth Stevens
PUBLISHING

BE A SUPER SPOTTER

Study these pictures and look out for them as you read this book. Can you answer the super spotter questions?

Which car can drive on water?

Which car has these headlights?

Which car has a door like this?

Which car is driving on logs?

Please visit our website, www.garethstevens.com. For a free color catalog of all our high-quality books, call toll free 1-800-542-2595 or fax 1-877-542-2596.

Published in 2025 by
Gareth Stevens Publishing
2544 Clinton St.
Buffalo, NY 14224

Designer: Paul Calver
Written by: Christiane Gunzi
Vehicle consultant: Gary Boyd-Hope
Editorial consultant: Mark Wilkinson

Photographs: A Touch of Class Limousines; Alamy; Ariel Motor Company Ltd; Bauer-Millett; Jamie Bell; F. Belley *www.photof1.com*; Glynne Bowsher; Bugatti Automobiles SAS; Caterpillar; Chrysler Group; DaimlerChrysler UK; DCUK Marketing Archive; Ford Motor Company; Steve Bailey, Gibbs Technologies; Simon Jagassar; Dave Jones at Santa Pod Raceway; Matt Jorgensen; Steve Jurvetson (under CC BY 2.0); Lamborghini; Land Rover; newlaunches.com; Robin Richardson; Kenneth D. Ringold; Rolls-Royce Motor Cars; Shutterstock.com (Art Konovalov, Artur_Nyk, betto rodrigues, Brostock, cristiano barni, EvrenKalinbacak, Fabrizio Annovi, Faiz Zaki, Foto by M, Gabriel Nica, GELEFIN, Gestalt Imagery, Jason Benz Bennee, Jay Hirano Photography, JBCarvalho Photography, Joel_420, Jose Breton - Pics Action, Kobby Dagan, luckyluke007, Mau47, Mike Mareen, Milan Rademakers, PuccaPhotography, Steve Lagreca, StoriesFromAnywhere, Supermop, Tomasz Szczecinski, VanderWolf Images, WildSnap); Mark Sims *www.rallygallery.com*; Truck Customs by Chris *www.f650pickups.com*; Volkswagen Group UK Ltd

Cataloging-in-Publication Data

Names: Gunzi, Christiane.
Title: Cars / Christiane Gunzi.
Description: Buffalo, NY : Gareth Stevens Publishing, 2025. | Series: Mega books
Identifiers: ISBN 9781482467932 (pbk.) | ISBN 9781482467949 (library bound) | ISBN 9781482467956 (ebook)\
Subjects: LCSH: Automobiles--Juvenile literature.
Classification: LCC TL147.G86 2025 | DDC 629.222--dc23

Printed in the United States of America

CPSIA compliance information: Batch #CSGS25: For further information contact Gareth Stevens at 1-800-542-2595.

CONTENTS

SPORTS CARS

These fast, exciting cars are sports cars. They have low, sleek bodies that sit close to the ground. The Lamborghini Huracán is named after a famous Spanish bull. Huracán means "hurricane" in Spanish. Sports cars cost a lot of money.

Ferrari 296 GTB

Ferrari

This Italian sports car is very fast, thanks to an electric motor that helps the gas engine. It is Ferrari's first plug-in, hybrid sports car.

Inside a Lamborghini

Lamborghini

This sports car is powered by a V10 engine and has a top speed of 201 miles per hour (mph) or 324 kilometers per hour (kph).

Porsche

This German car can go from 0 to 60 mph (96 kph) in less than four seconds. It has powerful brakes so it can stop quickly.

Which sports car is named after a famous bull?

HYPERCARS

Some sports cars are so fast and fantastic that only the richest people in the world can afford to buy them. These beautifully designed supercars and hypercars can cost more than $2 million and are very rare.

Can you point to?

wheel

rear spolier

badge

Bugatti Chiron

Koenigsegg Gemera

Koenigsegg

When this Swedish hypercar goes into production its plug-in hybrid V8 engine will make it the most powerful production car in the world!

How many McLaren F1 supercars were made?

Bugatti

This is one of the most expensive cars in the world. Only 500 Bugatti Chirons have been made.

McLaren Solus GT

McLaren

In 1994, McLaren produced one of the first modern supercars: the F1. Just 107 F1s were made. The Solus GT hypercar is one of the latest cars from McLaren, but unlike the F1 it can only be driven on a track.

The Bugatti Chiron has a sleek, streamlined body.

LUXURY CARS

World leaders, such as prime ministers and royalty, travel in large luxury cars. These cars are comfortable and powerful, and they are also very strong and can protect their passengers in case of an emergency or other danger.

Chrysler 300S

Chrysler

With its V8 Hemi engine, the Chrysler 300S offered power and comfort. Luxury four-door sedans like this and the 300C are being replaced by larger, more versatile Sports Utility Vehicles (SUVs).

Mercedes CLK55 AMG

Mercedes

This powerful car can go from 0 to 60 miles per hour (96 kph) in 5.1 seconds and has a top speed of 168 mph (270 kph). It has two exhaust pipes and can carry four people in luxury.

Can you point to?

badge

steering wheel

grille

Mercedes-Maybach

This German luxury concept car has appeared in a movie and a music video. It has four powerful electric motors and is almost 20 feet (6 m) long!

Vision Mercedes-Maybach 6

Which car has a mascot?

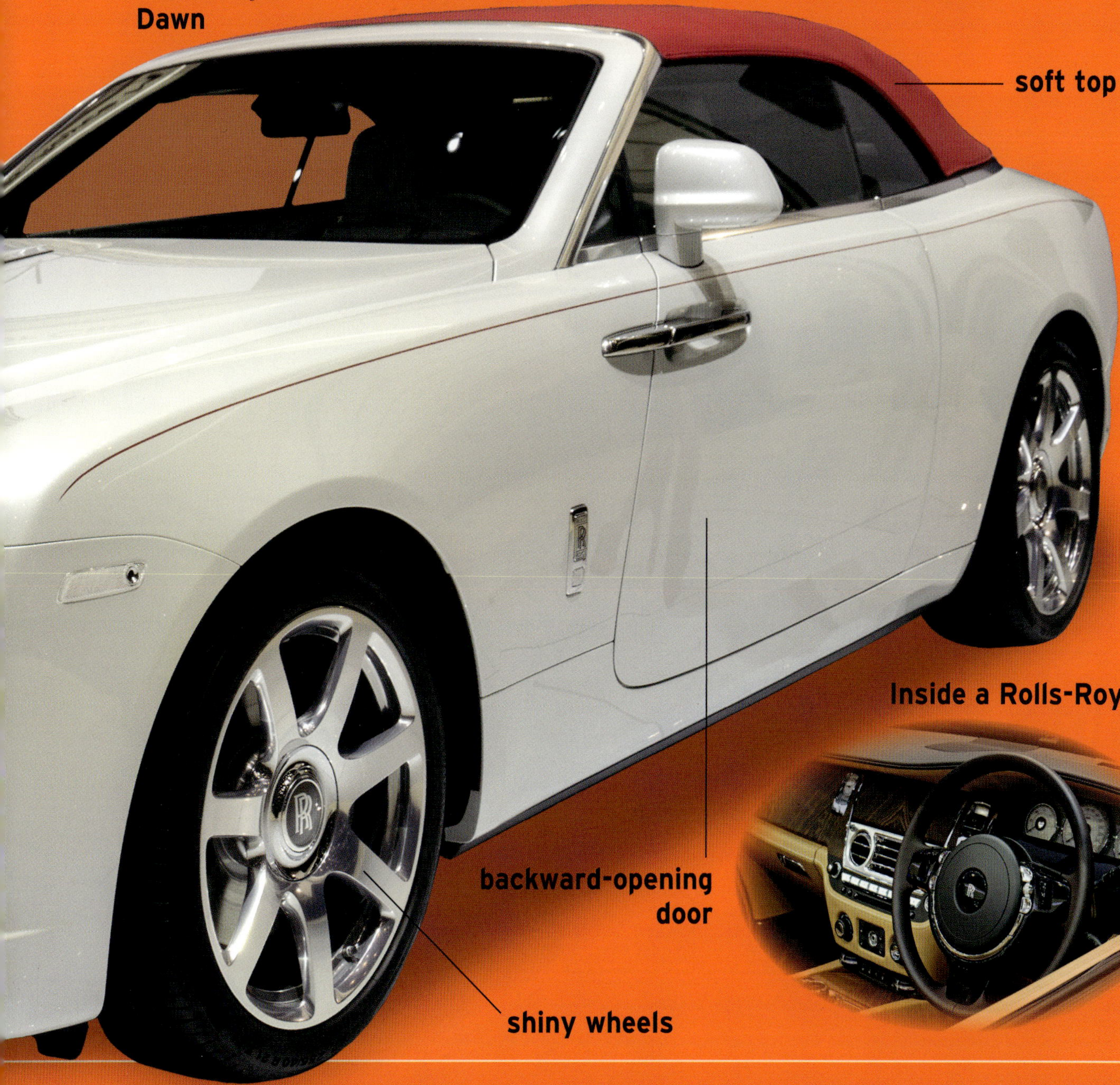

Rolls-Royce Dawn

Inside a Rolls-Royce

RACING AND RALLY CARS

Racing and rally cars are made with powerful engines and gearboxes. They also have extra features, such as roll cages, to keep the drivers safe. Racing takes place on a track, but rallies are on roads or cross-country.

Ford Puma Rally1

Ford

This Ford Puma is a plug-in hybrid, powered by a small gas engine and a powerful electric motor.

Which rally car has an electric motor?

Porsche RS Spyder

Aston Martin

The Aston Martin DBR9 was a very successful racing car, winning two Le Mans races in 2007 and 2008. It can go up to 195 mph (314 kph).

Aston Martin DBR9

Toyota

Toyota has been racing its Camry in famous NASCAR races since 2007. It has won 180 races in the Camry so far.

Toyota Camry

Porsche

Porsche won the 12 Hours of Sebring race in Florida with its RS Spyder racing car. Porsche cars have won the world famous 24 Hours of Le Mans race in France more than any other maker's cars.

FORMULA ONE

Motor racing is a fast, dangerous sport. Formula One cars race in competitions around the world called Grand Prix, which means "big prize." These cars cost millions of dollars to build. There is huge prize money for the winner.

The Grand Prix

In a Grand Prix race, drivers race each other around a track.

Ferrari

Driver Charles Leclerc's Formula One car was made in Italy by Ferrari. It has a Ferrari 066/10 engine with nine gears.

Ferrari SF-23

Mercedes-AMG F1 W14 E Performance

Mercedes-AMG

This Mercedes-AMG, like all Formula One cars, has a carbon fiber body. British drivers Lewis Hamilton and George Russell drove it in the 2023 championship.

Can you point to?

winglet

air intake

driver

Youngest Champion

This car was made by Red Bull Racing and driven by Sebastian Vettel from Germany. In 2010 he became the youngest Formula One champion ever at age 23.

Red Bull RB6

Red Bull

Max Verstappen won the 2023 Formula One World Championship in this RB19 car.

Where are Ferrari cars made?

Red Bull Racing RB19

DRAGSTERS AND HOT RODS

Hot rods are old cars that have had bigger engines added to make them go faster. Often they have wide tires and are painted bright colors. In drag racing, two dragsters race each other on a short, straight track. It is noisy and exciting to watch!

Ford Model A Coupé

Ford

The first hot rods were built out of old Ford cars. This one's engine has no cover.

1966 Chevrolet Chevelle SS

Chevrolet

This colorful car was made in 1966 and it has been painted red with flames at the front.

Can you point to?

rectangle

squares

circle

Dragster

Buick

This hot rod was made from an old car called a Buick. It has been painted blue and has an ornament on the hood.

Can you see a picture of a snake?

Dragsters

Dragsters are lighter and much more powerful than ordinary cars. They are incredibly fast. The fastest dragster can go from 0 to 338 miles per hour (544 kph) in less than four seconds.

4X4s

These big, strong vehicles are driven by all four wheels at the same time. A 4X4 can easily climb up steep slopes, drive through mud, and pull heavy loads. These powerful vehicles are often used on farms.

Can you point to?

lights

wing mirror

spare wheel

What colors are these 4X4s?

Land Rover

The first Land Rover 4X4 was developed over 75 years ago. Some Land Rovers have a snorkel so they can drive through deep water and mud.

Land Rover Discovery

Jeep Wrangler

Jeep

Jeep began making small 4X4s during World War II for soldiers to get around quickly. Modern Jeeps are much larger now.

Classic Land Rover Defender

A good grip

Jeeps, Land Rovers, and Hummers have powerful engines. They can drive over rocks, mud, ice, and snow, and up steep mountain tracks without slipping.

Jeep Commander

Hummer H2

snorkel

PICKUPS

These big, powerful pickup trucks are used by farmers and builders to do tough jobs. They can carry heavy loads and tow other vehicles. People also like to use pickup trucks because they are fun to drive.

Ford F650

This Ford pickup has a 300 horsepower engine. Some Fords have a special camera to help the driver see behind the vehicle when it is towing things.

Dodge Ram

This fast pickup can go from 0 to 60 miles per hour (96 kph) in five seconds. Its top speed is 154 mph (248 kph) and it has a 500 horsepower engine.

Dodge Ram SRT-10

alloy wheel

bumper

Which pickup is called the Dodge M80?

Dodge M80

Can you point to?

exhaust

wing mirror

wheel arch

Ford Model T

Ford created one of the first pickups over 100 years ago. They were often used on farms. Some were made with skis and tracks so they could deliver mail in heavy snow.

MONSTER TRUCKS

Around 50 years ago, a few people decided to make their pickups look more exciting. They added enormous wheels and called them "monster trucks." Many people now watch these mega vehicles race and do displays at shows.

Can you point to?

tire eyes teeth

Bigfoot

The owner of the first monster truck, Bigfoot, added huge tires to his Ford truck and then drove over some old cars in a field for fun.

Clever tricks

Drivers make their trucks do jumps. Some spin their truck in a circle. This is called a "doughnut."

Monstrous

Which was the first monster truck?

Swamp Thing

Car crusher

Monster trucks race each other, do jumps, and crush other vehicles by driving over them. They have special switches to turn off the engine if the driver loses control.

FUN CARS

Some cars are unusual and great fun. There are small electric ones, big, extra-long ones, brightly colored ones and a few cars that do not look like cars at all. One car even drives on water!

Mini Cooper

The Mini Cooper is a little car, so it is easy to park in cities. It has a top speed of 146 mph (235 kph), which is fast for such a small vehicle.

Ariel Atom

This car looks like a racing car but it can also travel on normal roads. It has no roof, doors, or windows.

Hummer H2

Stretch limos

Some limousines are big enough to have a party in and can be used to take a group of friends to special events, such as a wedding or a school dance.

Lincoln Town Car

Which fun car has no roof?

Can you point to?

triangle

circle

stripe

Bubble cars

Bubble cars are small, cheap, and fun to drive. This Microlino bubble car runs on electricity, making it good to use in cities.

Microlino

Aquada

This car can drive on land and on water. On the water, the wheels are hidden inside the car. It is fast enough to pull a water-skier!

Gibbs Aquada

ELECTRIC CARS

Until recently, most cars have used fossil fuels, such as diesel or gas. Electric vehicles have a large battery and use electric motors instead. They are quiet and produce no exhaust fumes, making them much cleaner. Hybrid cars use both an electric motor and a gas engine.

Charging

The batteries in today's electric vehicles need to be charged either at home or by plugging them in at public charging stations.

Nissan Leaf

charging station

Solar power

Getting power from the sun for the electric motor means that the car's battery can be smaller. Teams from universities compete in a race in Australia every two years to develop technology for solar-powered cars.

Durham University Electric Motorsport Ortus

streamlined cockpit

solar panels

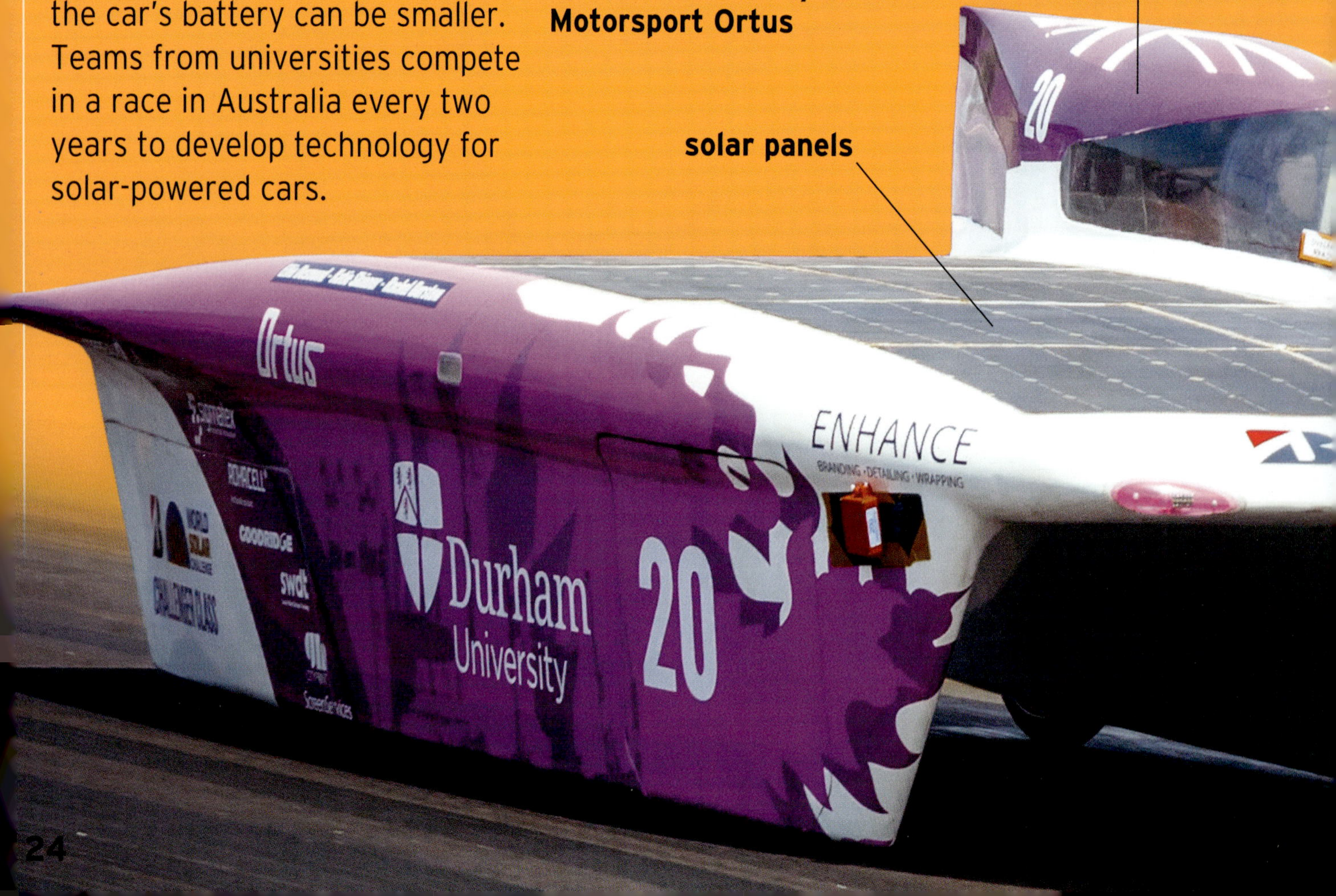

Powerful pickup

Tesla's futuristic electric pickup truck looks like something out of a science fiction movie. It is faster than many supercars and can go from 0 to 60 miles per hour (96 kph) in 2.6 seconds. The body is made from stainless steel panels that are cut into shape by lasers.

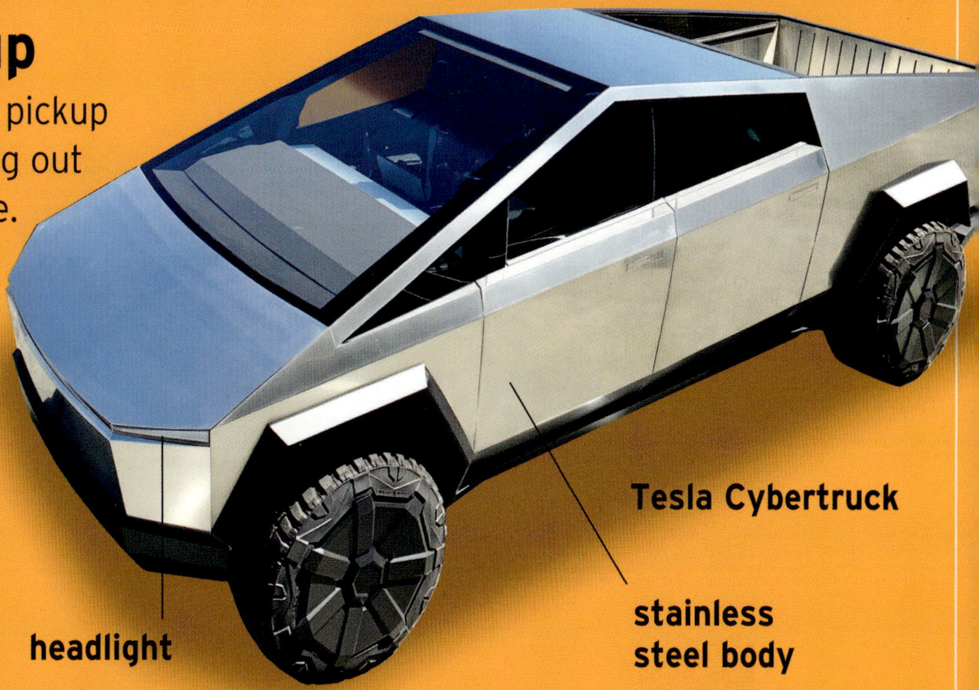

Which of these cars is powered by the sun?

Toyota Mirai

Fuel cell

Fuel cell cars like this Toyota Mirai don't need big batteries. They use hydrogen and oxygen to produce electricity to power their motor instead. They are very clean, giving off only water vapor and warm air.

Hydrogen fuel cell

CLASSIC CARS

When popular or unusual cars get old and are not made anymore, they sometimes become known as classic cars. These classics are usually rare and can be very expensive to buy. One day, some of the cars that we drive now may become classics too.

Beetle

This popular German car is the Volkswagen Type 1, but it is called the Beetle because of its shape.

Mustang

The Mustang was first built in the 1960s by Ford. Over one millon were sold in the first 18 months. The Mustang is the best-selling sports car in history.

Cobra

This AC Cobra was a fast British sports car in the 1960s. It had a big engine and a lightweight body.

Jaguar

The E-type Jaguar was a top sports car in the 1960s. Its design and sleek looks made it very exciting.

Lamborghini

This was one of the top Italian sports cars in the 1970s. Its doors have special hinges so they open upward.

Which cars have animal names?

Corvette

This car was built by hand in the 1950s. These fast cars were the first American sports cars.

SUPERFAST CARS

These superfast cars have jet engines. Thrust SSC is the fastest of them all and was driven by Andy Green, a jet fighter pilot. It was the first land vehicle to break the sound barrier.

Thrust going faster than sound

Thrust SSC

In October 1997, this supersonic car raced at 763 mph (1,228 kph) in the Black Rock Desert of Nevada. Thrust SCC has not been beaten yet.

Thrust SSC

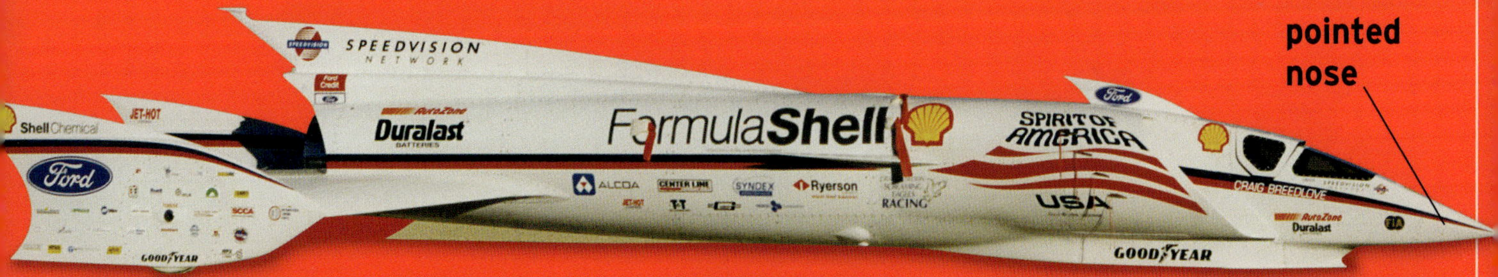

pointed nose

Spirit of America: Sonic Arrow

Spirit of America

This car is nearly 43 feet (13 m) long. It has five wheels and a turbojet engine. It reached 676 mph (1,008 kph) in the Black Rock Desert in 1996, but then it crashed.

Which is the fastest car of all?

tail fin

nose cone of Rolls-Royce engine

cockpit

Thrust 2

Thrust2

This British car has one Rolls-Royce jet engine. Thrust2 reached a speed of 633 mph (1,019 kph) in October 1983. It held the Land Speed Record from 1983 to 1997.

Thrust SSC's engines being tested

CARS OF THE FUTURE

Each year, millions of cars are made around the world, especially in China, the United States, India, Japan, Germany, and France. Designers sometimes create a whole new type of car. These imaginative designs are called concept cars.

Toyota Concept-i

AI assistance

The Concept-i has an AI system that reads people's emotions and helps them when they are driving.

Mercedes F 015 Luxury in Motion

Self-driving cars

Some cars will be like a living room on wheels. The steering wheel in this luxury concept car disappears into the dashboard when the car is driving itself.

AVTR car

This futuristic VISION AVTR concept car was inspired by the *Avatar* films. The low body shape and slim, advanced head and tail lights can now be seen on Mercedes' latest EQ electric cars.

Can you point to?

headlight

badge

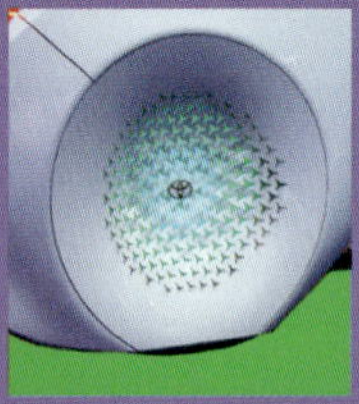

hidden wheel

Mercedes-Benz VISION AVTR

Back to the future

This sleek Vision One-Eleven electric concept car was inspired by Mercedes-Benz's C111 experimental car from the 1970s. Both cars have gullwing doors that open upward and bright orange paint.

Which concept car can tell how you feel?

GLOSSARY

AI - artificial intelligence. Computers use AI to observe things, make decisions, and work on their own to help people.

Alloy - a mix of two or more metals that is stronger and lighter than steel.

Carbon fiber - a material molded from tiny, thin strands of carbon that is very strong and very light.

Concept car - a unique vehicle used to display new car technologies or an idea of how a car might look in the future.

Fossil fuels - coal and oil from the ground that have been refined to make gas and diesel to power car engines.

Fuel cell - a fuel cell uses a chemical reaction between hydrogen and oxygen to produce electricity. It can be filled up with hydrogen much more quickly than charging an electric car's battery.

Gullwing doors - doors that open upward and outward, like a bird's wings.

Horsepower - a unit of measurement of mechanical power.

Hybrid - a car powered by both a gas engine and an electric motor. This makes it cleaner and helps it use less fossil fuel.

Le Mans - a 24-hour-long race is held at this French city's race track each year. It is a very tough challenge for drivers and their racing cars.

Plug-in hybrid - a hybrid car with a big battery that needs to be plugged in to charge it. These cars can run on electricity alone for short distances.

Roll cage - a strong metal framework to stop people inside a car from being crushed if it rolls over.

Solar panel - a sheet of light-sensitive silicon cells that generates electricity when sunlight shines on it.

Spoiler - a wing-shaped panel that helps to keep a car stable at high speed.

Streamlined - having a smooth, sleek shape that allows a car to move through the air more easily, making it faster and more economical.

INDEX